POSTCARDS

JAPAN

An Invitation

Beauty & Splendor

CHARLES E. TUTTLE COMPANY
Rutland, Vermont & Tokyo, Japan

These postcards, slightly larger than usual, require the same postage as a first-class letter.

Note: Names of Japanese follow the traditional order, surname first; others follow the Western order.

Published by the Charles E. Tuttle Co., Inc.
of Rutland, Vermont & Tokyo, Japan
with editorial offices at
2-6 Suido 1-chome, Bunkyo-ku, Tokyo 112

ISBN 0-8048-1731-6

First edition, 1991

Printed in Japan

The entrance gate to Kyoto's Komyoji shows Japan's autumn beauty at its finest.

From Japan: An Invitation, © *1991 by Charles E. Tuttle Publishing Co., Inc. Photo by Morita Toshitaka.*

Kinkakuji (Golden Pavilion) is one of Kyoto's most
popular attractions.

The lushness of May is clearly visible on the grounds of Kyoto's Sanzen'in, which dates from the 10th century.

From Japan: An Invitation, © *1991 by Charles E. Tuttle Publishing Co., Inc. Photo by Yasuda Narumi.*

The enigmatic rock garden of Ryoanji in Kyoto contains
15 stones in a sea of raked sand.

From Japan: An Invitation, © *1991 by Charles E. Tuttle*
Publishing Co., Inc. Photo by Morita Toshitaka.

Nara's Yakushiji is a temple dedicated to the Buddha of healing.

From Japan: An Invitation, © *1991 by Charles E. Tuttle Publishing Co., Inc. Photo by Morita Toshitaka.*

The path to Fushimi Inari Shrine in Kyoto is lined with hundreds of brightly painted gates.

From Japan: An Invitation, © *1991 by Charles E. Tuttle Publishing Co., Inc. Photo by Yasuda Narumi.*

Nikko's ornate Toshogu Shrine is the mausoleum of
Tokugawa Ieyasu, who unified Japan in 1600.

Japanese consider Itsukushima, Hiroshima Prefecture,
one of their country's three most beautiful sites.

From Japan: An Invitation, © *1991 by Charles E. Tuttle*
Publishing Co., Inc. Photo by J.O. Photo Agency.

Facing the Pacific Ocean, Iwate Prefecture's Rikuchu
coast is rugged and majestic.

Miyagi Prefecture's Matsushima, literally "pine islands," is a bay containing over 260 pine-covered islets.

From Japan: An Invitation, © *1991 by Charles E. Tuttle Publishing Co., Inc. Photo by Morita Toshitaka.*

The Kappa Bridge in Nagano Prefecture offers
spectacular views of the Japan Alps.

From Japan: An Invitation, © *1991 by Charles E. Tuttle
Publishing Co., Inc. Photo by Yasuda Narumi.*

At 12,385 feet, Mount Fuji is Japan's tallest mountain and its most famous site.

From Japan: An Invitation, © *1991 by Charles E. Tuttle Publishing Co., Inc. Photo by Morita Toshitaka.*

The ''wedded rocks'' off the coast of Ise, Mie
Prefecture, are joined by a sacred rope.

From Japan: An Invitation, © *1991 by Charles E. Tuttle
Publishing Co., Inc. Photo by Morita Toshitaka.*

Over 430 feet in height, Nachi Waterfall in Wakayama
Prefecture is one of the highest falls in Japan.

Blossoming cherry trees highlight the beauty of the
Inland Sea and a few of its more than 600 islands.

From Japan: An Invitation, © *1991 by Charles E. Tuttle
Publishing Co., Inc. Photo by Morita Toshitaka.*

Sakurajima in Kagoshima Prefecture is one of Japan's
most active volcanoes.

From Japan: An Invitation, © *1991 by Charles E. Tuttle
Publishing Co., Inc. Photo by Yasuda Narumi.*

Persimmons on a tree are the only remaining sign of
autumn in this scene of a Yamagata farmhouse buried
under snow.

From Japan: An Invitation, © *1991 by Charles E. Tuttle
Publishing Co., Inc. Photo by Yasuda Narumi.*

The village of Shirakawa, located deep in the mountains of Gifu Prefecture, is famed for its steeply roofed farmhouses.

From Japan: An Invitation, © *.1991 by Charles E. Tuttle Publishing Co., Inc. Photo by Morita Toshitaka.*

This weeping cherry tree is located on the grounds of
Heian Shrine, Kyoto.

From Japan: An Invitation, © *1991 by Charles E. Tuttle
Publishing Co., Inc. Photo by Frank Leather.*

An oarsman plies the waters of the Katsura River in the
Arashiyama district of Kyoto.

From Japan: An Invitation, © *1991 by Charles E. Tuttle
Publishing Co., Inc. Photo by Morita Toshitaka.*

The 37-foot Daibutsu (Great Buddha), cast in 1252, is one of Kamakura's most famous sites.

From Japan: An Invitation, © *1991 by Charles E. Tuttle Publishing Co., Inc. Photo by Morita Toshitaka.*

Osaka Castle, although destroyed and rebuilt several
times, is a symbol of the city.

From Japan: An Invitation, © *1991 by Charles E. Tuttle*
Publishing Co., Inc. Photo by Morita Toshitaka.

Moats and high walls surround the Imperial Palace,
located in the heart of Tokyo.

From Japan: An Invitation, © *1991 by Charles E. Tuttle
Publishing Co., Inc. Photo by Neil Krivonak.*